Rookie
Read-About®
Science

How Do You Know It's Spring?

by Lisa M. Herrington

Content Consultant

Randy C. Bilik, M.A.
Tulia A. Stark Elementary School, Stamford, Connecticut

Reading Consultant

Jeanne M. Clidas, Ph.D.
Reading Specialist

Children's Press®
An Imprint of Scholastic Inc.
New York Toronto London Auckland Sydney
Mexico City New Delhi Hong Kong
Danbury, Connecticut

Library of Congress Cataloging-in-Publication Data
Herrington, Lisa M., author.
  How do you know it's spring? / by Lisa M. Herrington.
    pages cm. — (Rookie read-about science)
  Summary: "Introduces the reader to the spring season."— Provided by publisher.
  Audience: 3-6.
  Includes index.
  ISBN 978-0-531-29947-0 (library binding) — ISBN 978-0-531-22576-9 (pbk.)
  1. Spring—Juvenile literature. I. Title. II. Title: How do you know it is spring?
III. Series: Rookie read-about science.
  QB637.5.H475 2014
  508.2—dc23   2013014927

Produced by Spooky Cheetah Press

© 2014 by Scholastic Inc.

Printed in China 62

SCHOLASTIC, CHILDREN'S PRESS, ROOKIE READ-ABOUT®, and associated logos are trademarks and/or registered trademarks of Scholastic Inc.

5 6 7 8 9 10 R 23 22 21 20 19 18 17 16 15

Photographs © 2014: Adam Chinitz: 30; age fotostock/Ron Rowan/YAY Micro/easyFotostock: 16, 31 top; Alamy Images: 7 (Bill Brooks), 23 (blickwinkel/Meyers); Dreamstime/Ginosphoto: 31 center bottom; Getty Images/Mark Hamblin/Oxford Scientific: 20; Glow Images/Kelly Funk: 27; Media Bakery: cover (Ariel Skelley), 4 (Ariel Skelley/Blend Images), 12 (Blend Images), 11 (Blue Jean Images), 24 (Cultura Limited); Shutterstock, Inc./Konstanttin: 8, 29, 31 bottom; Superstock, Inc./Steve Skjold/age fotostock: 28; Thinkstock/iStockphoto: 3 top, 3 bottom, 15, 19, 31 center top.

Table of Contents

4

Welcome, Spring!

Flowers bloom. Birds chirp and sing. Kites blow in the wind. That is how we know it is spring!

Daffodils, like the ones in this field, are some of the first flowers of spring.

These photos show a tree in all four seasons.

There are four seasons in each year. Each season lasts about three months. Spring is the season that comes after winter.

FUN FACT!

The first day of spring is March 20th.

Winter

Spring

Summer

Fall

What's the Weather?

In spring, the air gets warmer. The days are longer. That means it stays light in the evening for a longer time. The warm weather melts winter's snow and ice.

Crocus flowers are breaking through the last snow of winter.

Some spring days are sunny. Others are windy. We are ready to put our winter clothes away. Spring is in the air!

FUN FACT!

The seasons are opposite in the northern and southern parts of the world. When it is spring in the United States, for example, it is fall in Australia.

Grab your raincoat and umbrella! Spring brings the pitter-patter of rain. It also brings the roar of thunderstorms.

To measure how much rainfall you get this spring, try the experiment on page 30.

Plants and Animals in Spring

The warm, wet weather helps plants grow. Flowers pop up. New grass **sprouts**. Farmers plant their crops.

This farmer is using a tractor to plant seeds.

Buds form on trees. They open into leaves and flowers.

This photo shows flower buds and leaves on an apple blossom tree.

Animals are busy in spring. Bears and other animals awake from hibernation (HYE-bur-nay-shun), their long winter sleep.

Bears and their cubs leave their winter dens in spring.

Many birds **migrate** back from their warm winter homes. They build nests. They lay eggs and wait for babies to **hatch**. They bring their chicks food to eat.

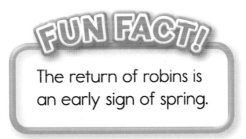

FUN FACT!

The return of robins is an early sign of spring.

Baby animals are born in spring.
Bunnies scamper in the woods.
Fuzzy ducklings splash in a pond.
The baby animals will grow big
and strong.

These baby bunnies are sticking close to their den.

This girl is helping her father plant vegetables in the garden.

Kids in Spring

In spring, we plant seeds in gardens. They will grow into vegetables and flowers.

FUN FACT!

In spring, we celebrate Earth Day on April 22nd. We learn how to care for our planet.

We spend more time outdoors. We ride our bikes. We have fun at the park.

This family is enjoying a bike ride on a beautiful spring day.

Let's Explore!

- Look at the picture. What do you see that tells you spring has arrived?

- Take a nature walk outside in spring. What clues can you find in your yard or neighborhood that say spring is here?

- In a science journal, draw pictures of what you observed. Write down some words that describe what you saw, heard, and smelled.

We play tennis and soccer.
What is *your* favorite thing to
do in spring?

Make a Rain Gauge

What You'll Need

- Plastic two-liter bottle
- Scissors
- Small rocks
- Tape
- Ruler
- Marker

Directions

1. Ask an adult to cut off the top of the bottle.

2. Place a few small rocks in the bottle to keep the wind from knocking it over.

3. Place the top upside down in the bottle. Tape it in place. Use a ruler and a marker to make inch marks on the bottle.

4. On the next rainy day, put the bottle in your yard. Measure how much water fell. Repeat the activity over several rainy days. Be sure to empty out the water each time.

5. Make a chart to track how much rain fell.

Think About It: On which day did it rain the most? On which day did it rain the least?

Glossary

buds (buhds): the parts of plants that grow into leaves or flowers

hatch (hach): when a baby animal breaks out of its egg

migrate (MY-grayt): to move from one place to another in search of warmth or food

sprouts (sprouts): begins to grow fast

Index

Facts for Now

Visit this Scholastic Web site for more information on spring:
www.factsfornow.scholastic.com
Enter the keyword **Spring**

About the Author

Lisa M. Herrington is a freelance writer and editor. Each spring, she looks forward to longer days, flowering trees and bushes, and the arrival of ducklings and goslings near her home. Lisa lives in Trumbull, Connecticut, with her husband, Ryan, and her daughter, Caroline.